The Mindbody Dictionary
WORKBOOK

Transform Old Patterns and
Facilitate Empowering Change

WRITTEN BY RONALD B. WAYMAN
WITH DENISE WAYMAN SCHOLES

Copyright © 2024 Mind Body Dictionary, LLC
All Rights Reserved

All rights reserved. No part of this book may be reproduced, stored in a retrieval system, or transmitted in any form or by any means, electronic, mechanical, photocopying, recording, or otherwise, without the prior written permission of the copyright owner, Ronald B. Wayman & Denise Wayman Scholes.

Mindbodydictionary.com

ISBN: 978-1-947176-04-1
Imprint: Independently Published

Created By
Ronald B. Wayman & Denise Wayman Scholes

Workbook Walk Through Videos

We have put together a series of videos to help deepen and expand your experience with this workbook. You can use this QR code or go to this web address and use the **password: MBDWorkbook*** to access and use these videos at your convenience.

MBDWorkbook*

https://mindbodydictionary.com/workbook-walk-through/

MBD Print Book | MBD on Apple iOS | MBD Google Play | Life Centering | MBD Classes | Mindbody Movements

WELCOME

INTRODUCTION

Welcome to the Mindbody Dictionary Workbook. The purpose of this workbook is to help facilitate a new process and routine in your life. One that will create a pattern of deepening your awareness, taking responsibility, empowering change, and transforming old patterns into aligned consciousness.

In this workbook you will find a more in-depth description of the 3 processes found at the beginning of the Mindbody Dictionary book. As you choose one or more processes for individual conditions, we hope you create a pattern that will help you to quickly discover personal insights related to your unique circumstance and needs, then release the stuck energies and emotions associated to the issue.

We wish you success and joy on your journey.

RON & DENISE

TABLE OF CONTENTS

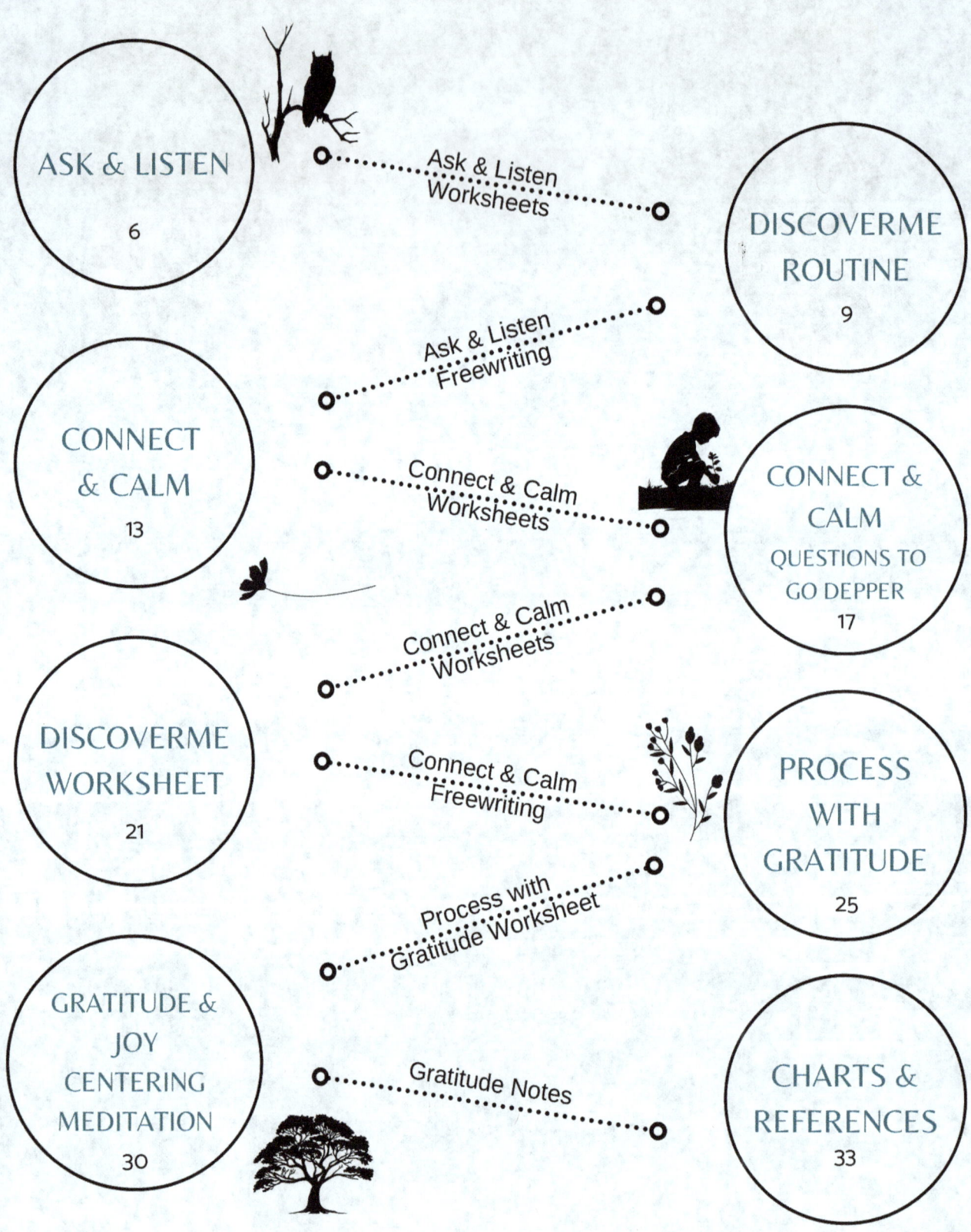

- ASK & LISTEN — 6
- Ask & Listen Worksheets
- DISCOVERME ROUTINE — 9
- Ask & Listen Freewriting
- CONNECT & CALM — 13
- Connect & Calm Worksheets
- CONNECT & CALM QUESTIONS TO GO DEPPER — 17
- Connect & Calm Worksheets
- DISCOVERME WORKSHEET — 21
- Connect & Calm Freewriting
- PROCESS WITH GRATITUDE — 25
- Process with Gratitude Worksheet
- GRATITUDE & JOY CENTERING MEDITATION — 30
- Gratitude Notes
- CHARTS & REFERENCES — 33

PATHWAYS TO HELP
THE PROCESS

OPTION
1

ASK & LISTEN | A basic pathway of seeking insight and understanding your body.

OPTION
2

Dive deeper into the source of your inner conflict connecting and calming the stress for greater wellbeing. | **CONNECT & CALM**

OPTION
3

PROCESS WITH GRATITUDE | Use the superpower of Gratitude to heighten spiritual awareness and deepen the healing process.

Ask and Listen
THE PROCESS

An Awareness

- Close your eyes.
- Take a deep cleansing breath.
- Calm the mind and allow messages from the body to flow up to the conscious mind.
- Ask, "What does my body want me to know about _____ condition?"
    - Write down what comes up in your mind, heart, or body.

Even if it seems random, consciously asking often yields answers. Listen. The messages may include memories, beliefs, words, emotions, images, or physical sensations.

Continue to ask questions to uncover the meaning of the messages. Write down your insights.

Once you understand the message, seek to release the energy, feeling, thought, etc. using the Connect and Calm or Gratitude Procedures. Repeat as often as desired.

Ideas to help you go deeper:

Consider the source:
- Belief
- Emotion
- Thought
- Decision
- Event
- Sensation

- *Find the specific belief.* You may free write or discuss with a trusted family member or friend to explore and discover the belief in relationship to the issue.
- *Discover the emotions.* Calm your mind and connect to your heart. Write down any emotions that surface. You may reference the emotions pages included in this workbook.
- *Observe your thoughts.* Did your mind go overactive or quiet? Was the information important or a distraction? Is your mind trying to rationalize, fix, hide, justify etc? If so, toss it.
    - Thank the mind for its desire to keep you safe, then release the erratic thoughts by refocusing on your breath.
    - If your mind said nothing, see if you can feel it in your heart or body.
- *Discover a decision.* What decisions could have been made around the troubled mindset?
    - Is there a decision that goes against your beliefs? Are your actions and values in conflict with one another?
- *Discover an event.* This could have been an event in childhood. It could have been yesterday.
    - Focus on your breath. Let your mind clear. Then watch and observe, see if a memory or a feeling enter into your awareness. Could that memory be related to your issue? If you don't know, ask. What do you feel or sense in response? Stay grounded in your breath.
- If the memory comes and you feel the stress again, breathe in and out any emotions, decisions, or pain associated with the memory. Allow your focus to stay stable as you release any attachment to the event. It's over now. Release it, embrace the learning experience and let it all go.
- You may try to envision yourself returning to that time and space with the wisdom you have now. Perhaps you offer yourself some support you didn't feel you had at the time. Perhaps you imagine angels or a sense of peace to guide you through the pain of the moment. Breathe, and release.

ASK & LISTEN WORKSHEET

What does my body want me to know?

What beliefs show up in relationship to this issue?

What emotions do I notice as I ponder on this issue?

What happened to my mind as I process or think about this?

What do I now choose to do with those thoughts?

ASK & LISTEN WORKSHEET

Thank you mind for...

....
....
....
....

What decisions do I recall around this issue?

....
....
....
....

Do I notice any decisions or beliefs that are in conflict with each other?

....
....
....
....

What are the details of an event that took place that may be related to this issue and/or the mental emotional conflict associated with it?

....
....
....

What do I notice in my body as I meditate on this event? (Tightness, tension, breathing changes, etc. Consider looking it up in the Mindbody Dictionary.)

....
....
....

Discoverme Routine
with Mindbody Dictionary

Optional Breathing Technique:

Repeat 3 times:
5 Deep, long breaths
3 Medium breaths
1 short breath

- I acknowledge the issue and underlying mindset.
- Breathe, focus on your breath.
- Bring your awareness to the issue with gratitude for the experience and with the intention of releasing.

Affirmations and Mindset:

- _____
- _____
- _____

Breathe each one in and out 3 to 5 times .

Notes: Thoughts   Beliefs   Memories

Release with Gratitude

ASK & LISTEN
FREE WRITING

Free write about the issue and any of the connected mindset and affirmations. You will know it is cleared when you are able to breathe in a relaxed state, and remain at peace, even while recalling the belief, past decision, or event.

Connect & Calm

The Process

- Look up the condition and read through the **Troubled Mindset**.
  - Choose two or three bullet point items that resonate, trigger, hurt or create curiosity for you the most. Write them down.
- Calm yourself as you observe.
  - Notice any tight muscles, breathe and relax each one.
  - Sit up, perhaps you stretch, put your feet flat on the ground, take a deep breath, root into the ground, imagine a waterfall helping your energy flow deep into the earth.
- Now focus on the area of your body or the condition that you are trying to tend to.
  - What does it feel like?
  - What do you notice?
- What are the *physical sensations*? Write it down.
- What are the *emotions* you experience as you pay attention to this condition? Write it down.
- What *thoughts* come to your mind? Even if they seem random, write them down, then observe a connection if present.
- Once you can see the personal resistance and the inner conflict more clearly, read the **Healing Mindset** page. Connect to what that coaching means to you.
  - What does the new mindset look like in your life, with this specific conflict?
  - What will you change in order to align with a higher vision?
- Choose two or three of your favorite Affirmations.
  - Write them on the affirmation page. perhaps you reference them once or twice each day, for as long as needed.
- Breathe in and out as you focus on the affirmation.
- Journal, align, release the old, replace with the new.
- Consciously choose your beliefs, observe any beliefs as they come to the surface, write them down. Clean out negative/harmful beliefs or belief patterns. Perhaps you clarify or deepen certain positive reinforcing beliefs.
- Consider the Healing Mindset and Affirmation pages to replace those beliefs.

*****

- Repeat the process.
- Sift through the Troubled Mindset as well as the other affirmations and concepts; does anything new stand out to you?
- Repeat the steps as many times as needed to feel aligned and connected. When you integrate these new beliefs into your heart and mind, they will naturally emerge anytime time you are faced with a question, challenge or relating issue.

CONNECT & CALM - THE PROCESS

Notes from observing my inner conflict:

....
....
....
....

What does my body/heart feel like?

....
....
....
....

What do I notice about my physical sensations?

....
....
....
....

Emotions I notice as I focus on this issue and it's connected mindsets:

....
....
....

Thoughts I notice as I focus on this issue and it's connected mindsets:

....
....
....

CONNECT & CALM - THE PROCESS

I wonder, what would this new mindset look like in MY life...

What changes to I imagine as I align with this new mindset?

CONNECT & CALM - THE PROCESS

My affirmations:

....

....

....

....

....

....

....

....

....

Some conflicting beliefs that emerge as I focus on these new affirmations are

....

....

....

....

....

I choose to believe..

....

....

....

Connect & Calm

Questions to help you go deeper:

Some Ideas

- When did this physical / mental / emotional problem begin? What was going on that hour, day, or week?
  - What were you thinking or feeling at that time?
  - Did any of those thoughts or feelings get stuck in your body?
- When do you notice yourself holding your breath throughout the day?
  - What thoughts, emotions, or memories are connected to those times?
- Where do you feel tightness in your body?
  - Focus on that area, do you see any colors, pictures, or movements in that area?
  - Do you feel any emotion as you focus on that area?
- What personal insights do you want to put in place of the old belief or emotion patterns that will better serve your well-being?
- Triggers:
  - Do you get tight when you make mistakes?
  - Do you shut down when it's extra loud or extra quiet?
  - Do you over or under react to certain words, actions, sounds, or smells?
- Forgiveness:
  - Do you need to forgive yourself or someone else?
    - Use the connect & calm or gratitude techniques
    - Simply say or write the words "I forgive you."
    - Give it to a higher power to resolve the balance of mercy or justice.
- Do you need to release any need for control?
- How does the internal change affect your experiences?
  - As you calm internally, are you able to trust in your life's experience?
  - As you release the old internally are you prepared to experience something new externally?
- Are there individuals, groups or ideas that you feel triggered by?
  - Bring your attention to them and use the connect and calm technique to retrain your body/mind to relax.

CONNECT & CALM - GO DEEPER

This issue began when...

....
....
....
....
....
....
....
....

I breathe differently when...

....
....
....
....
....

Some triggers I notice are...

....
....
....
....

CONNECT & CALM - GO DEEPER

I forgive myself for...

....

....

....

....

....

I forgive _____ for ....

....

....

....

....

....

I am grateful for.... ....

....

....

....

....

....

I release control of... ....

....

....

....

....

....

CONNECT & CALM - GO DEEPER

I imagine a radically new experience as I...

Discoverme Worksheet
with Mindbody Dictionary

Date: _____

Issue: _____

I Acknowledge a Troubled Mindset:
Releasing it with my breath.

- _____
- _____
- _____

I Embrace a Healing Mindset:
Assimilating it with my breath.

- _____
- _____
- _____

I Integrate these Affirmations:

- _____
- _____
- _____

Breathe each one in and out 3 to 5 times.

What thoughts or emotions do I notice?

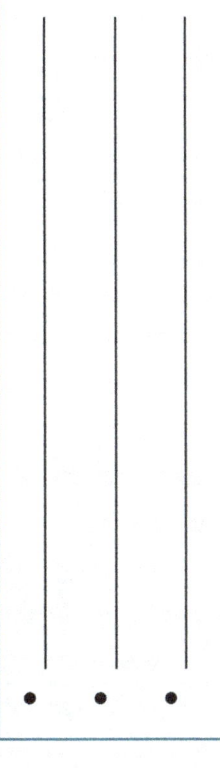

Anger / Sadness / Fear

Use your breath to bring the emotions to the surface & release.

Where do I feel or sense it physically?

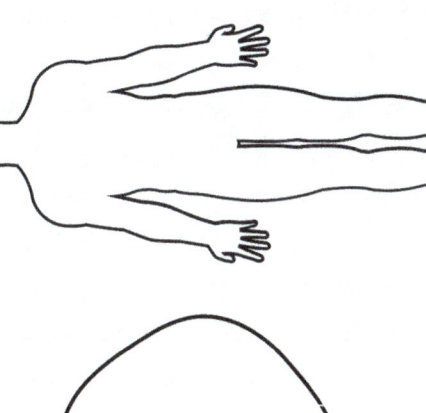

Breathe into, stretch, or move those areas of the body. Facilitate the release of stuck energy/emotion.

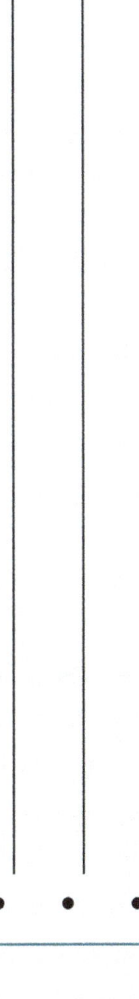

Mindbody DICTIONARY

CONNECT & CALM

FREE WRITING

Free write about the issue and any of the connected mindset and affirmations. You will know it is cleared when you are able to breathe in a relaxed state, and remain at peace, even while recalling the event.

Process with Gratitude

Procedure

- Notice an issue you are having with your body, mind, or heart.
- Read the **Troubled** and **Healing Mindsets** from the Mindbody Dictionary book or app.
- Write the thoughts and feelings you have about the negative and positive aspects of the condition.
- If needed, express or write your emotions to ensure that the part of you that feels wounded is honored. (If you are unsure about the emotional aspects or contributions to the condition, proceed anyway).
- The goal is not to wallow in pain and stubbornness of feeling horrible or wronged. The goal is to put those thoughts, scripts you tell yourself, attached emotions, fears of outcome, resentments, etc. in a space where you can observe them.
- Observing your problem with your reactions now gives you the next step.
- Reflect what you have done to deal with the problem and your reactions.
- Have you created space and time, to learn and grow from the problem?
- Have you found new character-building aspects in the process?
- If so, close your eyes and allow your heart and mind a moment to appreciate the value of the process of living this experience.
- Be grateful.
- If you need more time because you don't feel that you are learning at all or that your condition is hurting others, so you feel guilty – then you are holding onto the problem as if it is more important than growing from it.
- What is it that is more precious to you than finding peace inside?
- What is more valuable to you than finding amazing character-building attributes?
- What is more important than your ego and pride?
- Answer these and start to accept the possibility of finding value from your life experiences of negative and positive nature.
- Return to being grateful.

Questions to help you go deeper:

- What is the purpose of this life's experiences?
- Is there any value in holding on to pain or sorrow?
- Is there revenge or or need for justice getting in the way of gratitude?
- Is there a need for control or to "fix" things holding you back from learning, growing, and moving on?
- What do you value most about your experience?
- Who can you bless in your life from knowing and learning what you have?
- Do you feel extra compassion for others from your experiences?

PROCESS WITH GRATITUDE WORKSHEET

Thoughts and feelings about the mindset related to _____.

....

....

....

....

....

....

....

....

....

....

....

....

....

....

....

....

....

....

....

....

I observe and honor my thoughts and feelings.

PROCESS WITH GRATITUDE WORKSHEET

What is more precious to me than my health and wellbeing?

....

....

....

....

....

....

....

....

....

Is there anything more valuable than my inner state of peace?

....

....

....

....

....

What is actually more valuable than any ego or pride?

....

....

....

....

My courage is growing to face my life and those around me.

PROCESS WITH GRATITUDE WORKSHEET
GOING DEEPER

What is the purpose of this life's experiences?

Is there any value in holding on to pain or sorrow?

Is there revenge or or need for justice getting in the way of gratitude?

Is there a need for control or to "fix" things holding you back from learning, growing, and moving on?

What do you value most about your experience?

Who can you bless in your life from knowing and learning what you have?

Do you feel extra compassion for others from your experiences?

I love myself through my mistakes

This next meditation is taken directly from
"Life Centering with Breath and Awareness"
by Ronald B. Wayman

Gratitude & Joy Centering

This Gratitude and Joy centering is based on feelings and visualizations. It is combined with the energy emitted by the emotions of gratitude, joy, peace, euphoria and other positive power intents.

1. Relax, take a deep breath and slowly exhale.
2. Focus on the upper abdomen.
3. Breathe in with the intent of satisfaction. That satisfaction is flowing to this area of your body.
4. Pause, allowing the energy to flow freely.
5. Breathe out excess anxiety, tightness, worry and mistrust.
6. Pause.
7. Breathe in gratitude for your breath.
8. Breathe out all negative judgments, especially judgments that have led to resentments. Breathing out resentments releases links to your burdens.
9. Breathe in gratitude for the senses – taste, touch, feel, see, hear, smell, movement, gustatory and intuition.
10. Breathe out any negative thoughts.
11. Breathe in gratitude for the simple things of life.
12. Breathe out any negative feelings.
13. Breathe in gratitude for hope and how it feels in your soul.
14. Breathe out pain that others have caused you.
15. Breathe in understanding and appreciation for the wisdom developed from those painful experiences.

(Be creative – introduce your gratitude from your heart and soul) Continue with the gratitude cycle and then go to joy, peace, euphoria and other positive power intents.

The time to do the gratitude centering technique is not only when you want to feel good, like a cup of hot tea and a warm hug, but also when life has given you a couple of bumps that hurt. Gratitude brings back reality, resets, re-calibrates and helps restart your life without the pain of blame, criticism and resentment.

God gives us the abundance of life. We are such a blessed people. Compare your life to the lives of those who lived just two hundred years ago. The luxury that you now enjoy is greater than that of kings and queens of past eras. Be grateful that when you are able to express this understanding, you can see past the fog of daily life, and live a life beyond the confines of suppressing boundaries.

Your state of mind and heart determines your life experience.
Thank God daily for that awareness.

GRATITUDE NOTES

GRATITUDE NOTES

CHARTS & REFERENCES

ADDITIONAL PROMPTS TO CONSIDER

- On any prompt, ask one of these three questions:
  - Where in your body is that sitting?
  - What thoughts cycle because of that?
  - What behavior does it create?

- What is more important?
  - My way or being happy?
  - Making sure I am taken care of or the other person is taken care of?
  - My health or their health?
  - My job or my family?
  - Being Acknowledged or being safe?

I carefully approach each day with wisdom and understanding.

ADDITIONAL PROMPTS TO CONSIDER

- What am I avoiding when there is pain?
- What was I thinking?
- What part of my body always speaks pain or ache to me?
- What is the hidden message behind the pain?
- Does that message make me uncomfortable or relieved?
- Whats my pain?
- What's my concern?
- What consumes my thoughts?
- What's my result?
- Where's my intention?
- What's my intention?
- What muscles need my attention?
- What part of my body needs my care?
- What organ needs my breathing?
- What moves me? And what did I move?
- What am I fighting for?
- What am I running from?
- What do I wish for but have little hope of?

I carefully approach each day with wisdom and understanding.

ADDITIONAL PROMPTS TO CONSIDER

- What is the best discovery from the Mindbody Dictionary?
- What do you really want to accomplish with self-discovery and change?
- Can you find the keys to clarity and joy within the Mindbody Dictionary?

I carefully approach each day with wisdom and understanding.

GRATITUDE REFLECTION

NAME: DATE:

WHAT I AM GRATEFUL FOR TODAY

_____
_____
_____
_____

3 THINGS WHAT I LOVE ABOUT MYSELF

_____
_____
_____
_____

THE THINGS I CAN APPRECIATE ABOUT MY EXPERIENCE

_____
_____
_____
_____

www.mindbodydictionary.com

Discoverme Worksheet
with Mindbody Dictionary

Date: _____

Issue: _____

Where do I feel or sense it physically?

What thoughts or emotions do I notice?

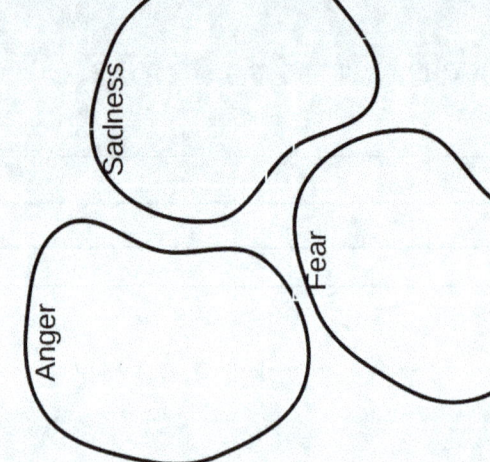
Anger | Sadness | Fear

Breathe into, stretch, or move those areas of the body. Facilitate the release of stuck energy/emotion.

Use your breath to bring the emotions to the surface & release.

I Acknowledge a Troubled Mindset:
Releasing it with my breath.

• _____
• _____
• _____

I Embrace a Healing Mindset:
Assimilating it with my breath.

• _____
• _____
• _____

I Integrate these Affirmations:

• _____
• _____
• _____

Breathe each one in and out 3 to 5 times.

Discoverme Worksheet
with Mindbody Dictionary

Date: _____

Issue: _____

I Acknowledge a Troubled Mindset:
Releasing it with my breath.

- _____
- _____
- _____

I Embrace a Healing Mindset:
Assimilating it with my breath.

- _____
- _____
- _____

I Integrate these Affirmations:

- _____
- _____
- _____

Breathe each one in and out 3 to 5 times.

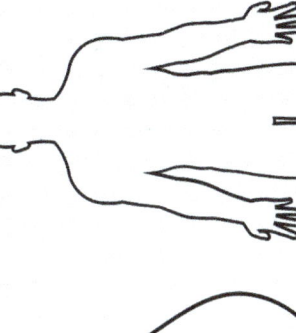

What thoughts or emotions do I notice?

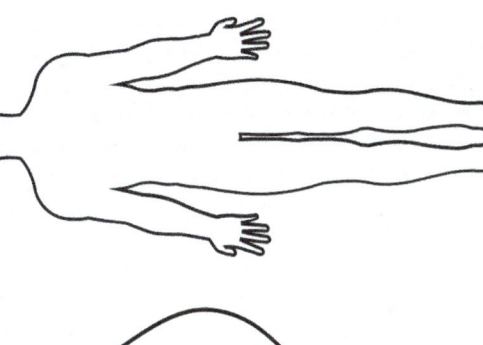

Anger | Sadness | Fear

Use your breath to bring the emotions to the surface & release.

Where do I feel or sense it physically?

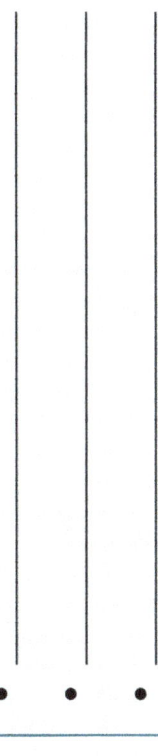

Breathe into, stretch, or move those areas of the body. Facilitate the release of stuck energy/emotion.

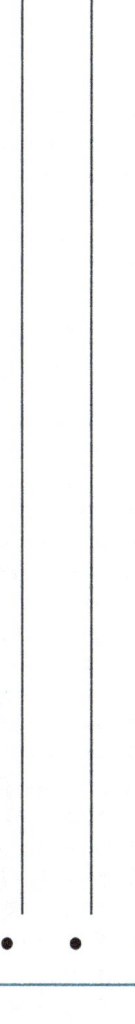

Mindbody DICTIONARY

Discoverme Worksheet
with Mindbody Dictionary

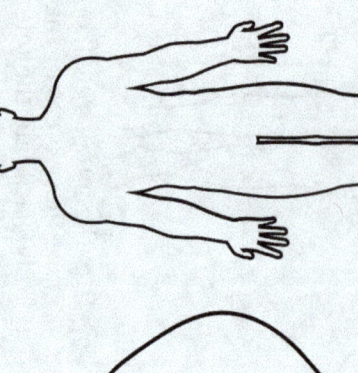

Date: _____

Issue: _____

Where do I feel or sense it physically?

What thoughts or emotions do I notice?

Anger Sadness Fear

I Acknowledge a Troubled Mindset:
Releasing it with my breath.

- _____
- _____
- _____

I Embrace a Healing Mindset:
Assimilating it with my breath.

- _____
- _____
- _____

Breathe into, stretch, or move those areas of the body. Facilitate the release of stuck energy/emotion.

Use your breath to bring the emotions to the surface & release.

I Integrate these Affirmations:

- _____
- _____
- _____

Breathe each one in and out 3 to 5 times.

Mindbody DICTIONARY

Discoverme Worksheet
with Mindbody Dictionary

Date: _____

Issue: _____

Where do I feel or sense it physically?

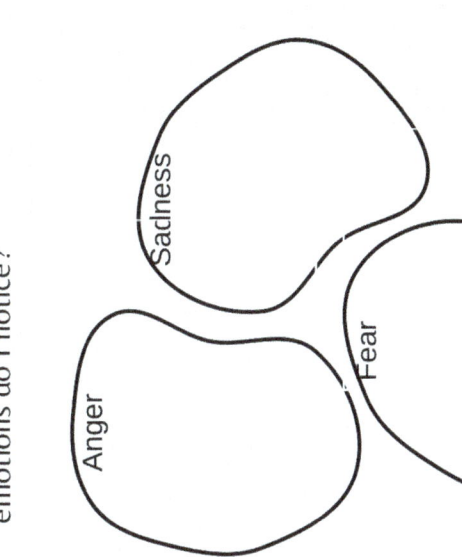

What thoughts or emotions do I notice?

- Anger
- Sadness
- Fear

Use your breath to bring the emotions to the surface & release.

Breathe into, stretch, or move those areas of the body. Facilitate the release of stuck energy/emotion.

I Acknowledge a Troubled Mindset:
Releasing it with my breath.

- _____
- _____
- _____

I Embrace a Healing Mindset:
Assimilating it with my breath.

- _____
- _____
- _____

I Integrate these Affirmations:

- _____
- _____
- _____

Breathe each one in and out 3 to 5 times.

Mindbody DICTIONARY

Discoverme Routine
with Mindbody Dictionary

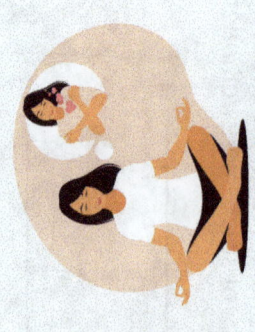

- I acknowledge the issue and underlying mindset.
- Breathe, focus on your breath.
- Bring your awareness to the issue with gratitude for the experience and with the intention of releasing.

Optional Breathing Technique:

Repeat 3 times:
5 Deep, long breaths
3 Medium breaths
1 short breath

Affirmations and Mindset:

-
-
-
-

Breathe each one in and out 3 to 5 times.

Notes:

Thoughts

Beliefs

Memories

Release with Gratitude

Discoverme Routine
with Mindbody Dictionary

Optional Breathing Technique:

    Repeat 3 times:
    5 Deep, long breaths
    3 Medium breaths
    1 short breath

- I acknowledge the issue and underlying mindset.
- Breathe, focus on your breath.
- Bring your awareness to the issue with gratitude for the experience and with the intention of releasing.

Affirmations and Mindset:

- _____
- _____
- _____
- _____

Breathe each one in and out 3 to 5 times .

Notes: Thoughts   Beliefs   Memories

Release with Gratitude

Discoverme Routine
with Mindbody Dictionary

- I acknowledge the issue and underlying mindset.
- Breathe, focus on your breath.
- Bring your awareness to the issue with gratitude for the experience and with the intention of releasing.

Optional Breathing Technique:

Repeat 3 times:
5 Deep, long breaths
3 Medium breaths
1 short breath

Affirmations and Mindset:

- _____
- _____
- _____
- _____

Breathe each one in and out 3 to 5 times.

Notes:

Thoughts

Beliefs

Memories

Release with Gratitude

Discoverme Routine
with Mindbody Dictionary

- I acknowledge the issue and underlying mindset.
- Breathe, focus on your breath.
- Bring your awareness to the issue with gratitude for the experience and with the intention of releasing.

Optional Breathing Technique:

Repeat 3 times:
5 Deep, long breaths
3 Medium breaths
1 short breath

Affirmations and Mindset:

- _____
- _____
- _____
- _____

Breathe each one in and out 3 to 5 times .

Notes: Thoughts   Beliefs   Memories

Release with Gratitude

EMOTION REFERENCE CHARTS

Fear
- Nervous
- Worry
- Terror
- Phobias
- Rejected
- Betrayed
- Anxious
- Overwhelmed
- Unsteady
- Controlling
- Insecure
- Obsessed

Anger
- Frustrated
- Rage
- Irritation
- Annoyed
- Agitated
- Bitter
- Judgemental
- Defensive
- Critical
- Greed
- Forceful
- Grudge

Sadness
- Grief
- Loneliness
- Depressed
- Heavy
- Hopeless
- Hurt
- Worthless
- Guilt
- Can't let go
- Apathy

Transformation	Unfolding Spiritually	Pious	Apathy
Power	Awakening	Spiritual Addiction	Learning Difficulties
Insight	Divine Support	Confused	Afraid to Trust
Wisdom	Purpose	Not Curious	Divine Support
Gratitude	Union	Hiding	Anger to God
Trust	Accepting of Others	Disconnect	
Hope	Inspired	Depressed	Disillusioned
Calm in action	Thoughtful	Heaviness	Overwhelmed
Clarity	Insight	Speech	Uptight
Faith in life	Spiritual	Anxious	Sleep issues
Flexible	Purpose	Confused	Headaches
Focused	Intuition	Hurried	Obsesed
Healing	Respect	Sadness	Interrupts
Hope	Faith in others	Loneliness	Anger
Discernment	Creative	Opinionated	Critical
Communication	Listening	Lies	Overwhelm
Speech	Energy	Gossips	Stifled
Speaking Truth	Energetic	Suppression	Smothered
Caring/Kind	Compassionate	Grief	Fear
Understanding	Lovable	Betrayed	Rejected
Full of Love	Empathic	Conditional Love	Bitter
Open and Warm	Forgivness	Hopeless	Co-Dependency
Sincere	Faith in Self	Hurt	Jealousy
Balanced	Sensory	Self-Blame	Poor Boundaries
Strength	Trusting Others	Controlling	Forceful
Courage	Inter-relational	Fear	Poor Personal Boundaries
Balanced Empathy	Confident	Dictator	Power of Powerless
Nourishing Self	Humor	Demanding of Respect	Pleaser
Capable	Trust	Manipulative	Worries
Good Enough	Helpful	Rebellious to Dictator	Need for Punishment
Creative	Faith in the process	Ungrounded	Obsessive Attachment
Fun	Start & Complete Projects	Destructive	Blame Others
Cleanliness	Pleasure	Shame/Worthlessness	Guilt
Pure	Balanced Elimination	Desire to Control	Emotionally Dependent
Emotional Intelligence	Flexibility	Addiciton to Pleasure	Entitled
Healthy Boundaries	Self-Nurturing	Oversensitive	Can't Let go
Movement	Grounded	Anger	Greed
Life	Feeling Accepted	Danger	Not Feeling Accepted
Blood / Good Health	Prosperity	Fear / Worry	Weak Consitution
Confident	Family	Focus Inward	Trip Easily
Faith in the Earth	Vitality / Stability	Selfish	Phobias
Safe	Able to Relax	Terror	Disorganized

RONALD B. WAYMAN

DENISE WAYMAN SCHOLES

www.mindbodydictionary.com

Ron has devoted the past three decades to passionately coaching individuals to empower their inner storyline to become their best selves.

He teaches many classes and wrote a brain integration and mindfulness self-help book called Life Centering. He enjoys teaching Life Centering techniques to family, friends, and clients.

Denise's journey into Energy Healing awakened a passion for understanding, listening, and aligning with the insights provided by our bodies.

She applies her Empowerlife studies to guide clients nationwide towards greater connection, healing, and alignment.

mindbodydictionary@gmail.com

https://www.instagram.com/mbdictionary/

www.mindbodydictionary.com

https://www.facebook.com/mindbodydictionary

www.ingramcontent.com/pod-product-compliance
Lightning Source LLC
Chambersburg PA
CBHW081433070526
44586CB00020B/2568